<u>Bi</u>

James Egan was born in 1985 and lived in Portarlington,
Co. Laois in the Midlands of Ireland for most of his life.
In 2008, James moved to England and studied in Oxford.
James married his wife in 2012 and currently lives in
Havant in Hampshire.
James had his first book, 365 Ways to Stop Sabotaging
Your Life, published in 2014.
Three of James' books have become No.1 Best Sellers -
365 Things People Believe That Aren't True, Another 365
Things People Believe That Aren't True and 500 Things
People Believe That Aren't True.

1,000 Facts about Animated Films

by

James Egan

ISBN: 978-1-326-50309-3

Lulu Publishing Services rev. date: 11/12/2015

Dedicated to
Nathan "Brakes" Turtle

Content

101 Dalmatians
1961

1. If this film didn't do well, Disney would've had to shut down its animation studio.

2. Of the fifteen puppies that Perdita gives birth to, only six are named – Patch, Penny, Pepper, Freckles, Lucky and Rolly.

3. The story was written by Dodie Smith. Her Dalmatians had fifteen puppies. Like the film, one of the puppies was lifeless but her husband revived it.

4. When 101 Dalmations was released, it was the most successful animated film ever.

5. Every musical Disney film has at least three songs except for this one, which only has two.

6. Clarence Nash provided the barks in the film. He is most famous for providing the voice of Donald Duck.

7. The dogs from Lady and the Tramp make a cameo.

8. Mickey Mouse appears throughout the film as a pattern on the Dalmatians.

9. Walt Disney was so unhappy with the animation, that he never forgave the lead animator until his dying day.

10. Someone counted all of the black spots in the film, frame-by-frame and reached the grand total of 6,469,952.

A Bug's Life
1998

11.   When the director heard that DreamWorks were making a film about ants (called Antz,) he thought they were making this film and he was about to be fired.

12.   Hopper's walk and gestures are modelled on Steve Jobs.

13.   The pizza van from Toy Story can been seen straight after the circus scene.

14.   This is the first PIXAR film to have outtakes.

15.   The film's trailer has scenes which aren't in the film. This became a PIXAR trademark.

16.   The names on the boxes in The City are the names of the writers' kids.

17.   The title was originally going to be Bug Story.

18.   Robert De Niro turned down the role of Hopper.

19.   A short film was shown in the cinemas just before A Bug's Life called Geri' Game. PIXAR have shown a short before all of their films ever since.

20.   Although the villains are grasshoppers, the animators said their movements are based on locusts. Clearly, the animators didn't realise that locusts and grasshoppers are the same species. A locust's biological name is short-horned grasshopper.

21.   Woody from Toy Story cameos in the outtakes.

A Christmas Carol
2009

22.   Christopher Lloyd was considered for the role of Scrooge.

23.   This was the first Disney film that starred Jim Carrey.

24.   The story is based in 1843.

25.   This story involves a lot of time travel. This film was directed by Robert Zemeckis, who directed Back to the Future, the most famous film ever about time-travel.

26.   Michael J. Fox was considered for a role.

27.   Gary Oldman and Lesley Manville play Mr. and Mrs. Cratchit. They were married in real life.

28.   Scrooge is fifty-seven.

29.   Gary Oldman plays Marley, Bob Cratchit and his son, Tiny Tim.

30.   A picture of Charles Dickens can be seen in the Cratchit home above the fireplace.

31.	This is one of the most accurate versions of A Christmas Carol. Although scenes were added that were not in the original story, most of the dialogue is word-for-word the same as the Dickens' classic.

A Nightmare Before Christmas
1993

32.   Tim Burton came up with the story when he saw Halloween decorations being torn down from a shop and being replaced with Christmas decorations.

33.   Disney strongly considered making a sequel.

34.   Tim Burton considered making this a tv special.

35.   Behemoth is based on the B-movie actor and wrestler, Tor Johnson.

36.   Jack delivers a snake to kids which looks exactly like the sandworm in the film, Beetlejuice.

37.   Sally's insides are made of leaves.

38.   Elvis-plates can be seen in the first house that Jack Skellington visits. This is a reference to Elvis' song, Blue Christmas.

39.   The trailer said that this was a Disney film even though it wasn't.

40.   Tim Burton made up the story when he was a teenager. In his first draft, there were only three characters – Jack, Zero and Santa.

41.   This was supposed to be a Disney film but it was considered too scary.

The Adventures of Ichabod and Mr. Toad
1949

42.   The original title was Two Fabulous Characters.

43.   Ichabod Crane's story is based on the 1820 tale, The Legend of Sleepy Hollow.

44.   Brom Bones' name is actually Abraham Van Brunt.

45.   Brom Bones' real name means "exalted father."

46.   Brom Bones became the inspiration for Gaston in Beauty and the Beast.

47.   Ichabod Crane's face, body, walk and gestures are based on the movements of a crane bird.

48.   Crane's horse is called Gunpowder.

49.   The song, Headless Horseman, was nearly cut from the film for being too disturbing. It is considered the scariest song in Disney history.

50.   Brom Bones' horse is called Daredevil.

51.   The Headless Horseman is considered the scariest villain in Disney history. Disney still get complaints about the character to this day.

52.   Toad's full name is J. Thaddeus Toad.

The Adventures of Tintin:
The Secret of the Unicorn
2011

53.   This is the first animated film directed by Steven Spielberg.

54.   The story is based on three of the Tintin comics – The Crab with the Golden Claws, The Secret of the Unicorn and Red Rackham's Treasure.

55.   Jack Nicholson was considered for Haddock.

56.   This is the first comic book adaptation made by Steven Spielberg.

57.   The painter in the beginning is based on Herge, the creator of Tintin.

58.   This is the first 3D film directed by Spielberg.

59.   Meryl Streep was considered for Bianca.

60.   Leonardo DiCaprio was considered for Tintin.

61.   Billy Crystal was considered for Professor Calculus.

62.   This is the first film to win the Golden Globe Award for Best Animated Picture that wasn't made by PIXAR.

Aladdin
1992

63.   The man who introduces the film is actually the Genie. Not only does he have the same beard and clothes but they are also the only characters that have five fingers. On top of that, they are both voiced by Robin Williams.

64.   This was the first film where the advertisements emphasised one of the lead actor (Robin Williams) as a selling point.

65.   Robin Williams improvised sixteen hours of material for his role as the Genie.

66.   Robin Williams improvised so many lines, that the film got turned down for a Best Adapted Screenplay Oscar nomination.

67.   The actor who plays Jafar, Jonathan Freeman, is scared of parrots.

68.   Patrick Stewart was supposed to play Jafar.

69.   The Genie impersonates Jack Nicholson, Rodney Dangerfield, Groucho Marx, Arnold

Schwarzenegger, Robert De Niro and many, many more.

70.   Since the Genie makes many references to modern times (Robert De Niro, Jack Nicholson) some Disney fans theorize that the story doesn't take place in the past but actually in the far distant future.

71.   The opening scene with the merchant was unscripted. The scene was prepared by asking Robin Williams to stand behind a table, which had many objects on it that were covered by a bed sheet. Williams had no idea what was underneath the bed sheet so when he took it off, he had to improvise with what he saw as his character. 90% of his lines were considered inappropriate for children.

72.   Every time Aladdin lies while he is dressed as a prince, the plume on his hat falls and covers his face.

73.   Mickey Mouse' head appears briefly on Rajah' head during his second transformation.

74.   Danny DeVito was considered for the role of Iago.

75.   Robin Williams' last line is, "Made you look." This is also his last line in the film, Good Morning, Vietnam.

76.   When the Genie sings, Friend Like Me, he mentions "Scheherazade had her thousand tales." Scheherazade was the story-teller of A Thousand and One Arabian Nights. One of these stories was Aladdin.

77.   Aladdin was modelled on Tom Cruise.

78.   Jafar's voice is based on Boris Karloff and Vincent Price.

79.   John Candy was considered for role of The Genie.

80.   Eight songs were removed from the final cut.

81.   While Steven Spielberg was making Schindler's List, he would call Robin Williams when he was making this film. He would put Williams on loudspeaker and

Williams would tell jokes to the entire cast and crew of Schindler's List.

82.   Jafar's face is based on Maleficent from Sleeping Beauty.

83.   During the Whole New World scene, Aladdin and Jasmine fly over Japan and Greece. The designs of the buildings were used again for the films, Hercules and Mulan.

84.   Robin Williams had a massive falling out with the film and he refused to return for the sequel, The Return of Jafar.

85.   The film spawned a television show in 1994. Since Robin Williams didn't want to have anything to do with it, Dan Castellanta played the Genie. Castellanta is most famous for providing the voice for Homer Simpson in The Simpsons.

86.   Disney eventually apologised to Robin Williams and he agreed to return as the Genie in the sequel, Aladdin and the King of Thieves.

Alice in Wonderland
1951

87.   This film has more songs than any other Disney film.

88.   The film was in development for ten years. It took another five years to make.

89.   Alice in Wonderland made very little money and nearly bankrupted Walt Disney.

90.   The Doorknob is the only character in the film that wasn't in the original story.

91.   The Mad Hatter is actually called The Hatter. The Cheshire Cat says he's mad but doesn't name him.

92.   The film is based on two of Lewis Carroll's books – Alice's Adventures in Wonderland and Through the Looking Glass.

93.   According to the writer, Lewis Carroll, he created the story to show how absurd mathematics is.

94.   The March Hare is called Haigha.

95.   The only character that is in the original story that wasn't in the film was Mock Turtle.

96.   This film has more speaking characters than any other Disney film.

All Dogs Go to Heaven
1989

97.   The film was inspired by It's a
Wonderful Life.

98.   The title comes from a quote by Robert
Louis Stevenson, the writer of Treasure
Island.

99.   Steven Spielberg was supposed to be the
film's producer.

100.   There is a scene that seems to come out
of nowhere involving a singing Big Lipped
Alligator. This scene has popularised the
phrase, "Big Lipped Alligator Moment,"
which is a scene in any film that has no
build-up or connection to the plot and is
never mentioned again. The term was
popularised by film critic, Doug Walker, on
his show, The Nostalgic Critic.

Antz
1998

101.   This is DreamWorks' first animated film.

102.   Arnold Schwarzenegger turned down the role of Weaver. It went to Sylvester Stallone.

103.   Christopher Walken was only meant to have a small part but he was so entertaining when he recorded his lines, that his role was expanded.

104.   This was the second computer-animated film ever. The first was Toy Story.

105.   The film depicts a war against ants and termites. Although termites are shown to be superior, ants would win in a fight as they would easily outnumber them.

106.   No human faces are shown in the film as the special effects weren't good enough for the time.

107.   Woody Allen wrote some of the screenplay.

108.   The story is loosely based on Aldous Huxley's, Brave New World.

109.   In the original script, the ants wore clothes and gloves.

110.   Woody Allen did all of his dialogue as Z in five days.

The Aristocats
1961

111.   The Aristocats was supposed to have a
sequel but it was scrapped.

112.   The story was intended as a two-part,
live-action television series.

113.   The Chinese Cat's lines in Ev'rybody
Wants to Be a Cat were removed from the
soundtracks for being politically incorrect.

114.   This was the last film to be approved by
Walt Disney.

115.   This was the first film completed by the
Disney studio after Walt Disney's death.

Atlantis: The Lost Empire
2001

116. Marc Okrand created the Atlantean language. He also invented the Vulcan and Klingon languages in Star Trek.

117. Tim Curry was considered for the Atlantean king.

118. The crew wore t-shirts that said, "Fewer songs, more explosions."

119. This is one of the only Disney films that says what year it takes place in – 1914.

120. Milo is the first male lead in a Disney animation to wear glasses.

121. Tommy Lee Jones was considered for Commander Rourke.

122. Kurt Russell was considered for a role.

Bambi
1942

123.   This was the first mainstream animated film where children did the voices of the young characters. Normally, adult actors would mimic children to play younger characters but Disney wanted the voices to sound genuine.

124.   Thumper the rabbit was supposed to be called Bobo.

125.   Two asteroids have been named Bambi and Thumper.

126.   The animators said that the hardest thing to animate in this film was the antlers of Bambi's father.

127.   Humans are never seen in the film.

128.   "Man is in the forest" was a code that Disney employees would use when Walt Disney was coming down the hallway while making this film.

129.   The deer that Bambi fights is called Ronno.

130.   This is the first Disney film where none of the songs are sang by any of the characters.

131.   Some scenes of the woodland creatures and forest fire are actually unused footage from the film, Pinocchio.

132.   Donnie Dunagan played Young Bambi. He became a Marine and the youngest drill instructor in history and eventually became a Major in the Vietnam War. He never told anyone that he voiced Bambi during the war because he was afraid that he would get bullied.

133.   The film is based on the 1923 story, Bambi, A Life in the Woods.

134.   The original story had a sequel called Bambi's Children.

135.   In the original script, the hunter was supposed to die in the forest fire. This would then show Bambi that humans were not all-powerful.

136.   In one of the early scripts, it was Bambi who would be shot, not his mother.

137.   This was the last animated Disney film for eight years. This was because most of the animators were in the military during World War II.

Beauty and the Beast
1991

138.   The Prince was eleven years old when the enchantress turned him into the Beast.

139.   The stained-glass window in the prologue has the Latin phrase, "Vincit qui se vincit." It means, "He conquers, who conquers himself."

140.   Rupert Everett auditioned for Gaston but didn't get the role because he didn't sound arrogant enough. He remembered this when he auditioned for Prince Charming in Shrek 2. He got the part.

141.   The roars that Beast makes are from a mix of big cats but mainly a lion.

142.   Angela Lansbury (who voiced Mrs. Potts) asked the director to get somebody else to sing the song, Beauty and the Beast, as she believed she wasn't good enough. The director asked her to make one recording as a backup. That recording ended up in the film.

143.   Chip is the only member of Beast's staff that calls Belle by her name.

144.   Gaston's sidekick is called Le Fou. It means "idiot" in French.

145.   In The Mob Song, Gaston sings, "Screw your courage to the sticking place." This is a line from Shakespeare's play, Macbeth.

146.   Julie Andrews was considered for Mrs. Potts.

147.   This was the first animated film to be nominated for a Best Picture Oscar.

148.   According to the writer, the character of Belle was inspired by Katherine Hepburn.

149.   This film was so successful that the Oscars created the Best Animated Feature category the following year.

150.   Patrick Swayze was considered for Gaston.

151.   Tim Curry was considered for Beast.

152.   Be Our Guest was supposed to be sung by Maurice.

153.   Maurice's socks never match in any scene.

154.   John Cleese was considered for Cogsworth.

155.   David Ogden Stiers voiced Cogsworth. He originally auditioned for Lumiere.

156.   This was the first animated film to win a Golden Globe for Best Picture.

157.   Belle is the first brown-haired Disney princess.

158.   In the very last shot of Gaston, skulls can be seen in his eyes for a split-second.

159.   Near the end of the film, Gaston screams, "Belle is mine!" When he says this, he is mouthing, "Time to die!" This sentence was changed at the last minute to "Belle is mine!" because the studio didn't want the word "die" in a children's film.

160.   Paige O' Hara was in her thirties when she voiced the seventeen-year-old Belle.

161.   Jackie Chan played the Beast in the Chinese dub.

162.   Paige O' Hara sobbed genuine tears when she recorded Belle's final scene. Afterward, the director asked her if she was ok. She shouted, "Acting!"

163.   Belle's blue-and-white dress is based on Dorothy's dress in The Wizard of Oz.

164.   Regis Philbin auditioned for Beast.

165.   Glen Keane spent two weeks animating the Beast's transformation scene. He said it was the highlight of his career.

166.   Belles final dance with the Prince is recycled animation from Princess Aurora and Prince Phillip in the film, Sleeping Beauty.

167.   Belle is the only character in her hometown that wears blue.

Bee Movie
2007

168. Barry and other male bees have stingers. In real life, only female bees have stingers.

169. Jerry Seinfeld came up with the title as a joke to Steven Spielberg. Spielberg loved the idea and encouraged Seinfeld to make it into a film.

170. The story was originally going to be live-action.

171. The film's fake title was Flowers.

172. Barry owns hundreds of sneakers. The actor who plays Barry, Jerry Seinfeld, owns 500 sneakers in real life.

173. Despite what is shown in the film, male bees don't make honey.

Big Hero 6
2014

174. Baymax's movements are based on a baby with a full diaper.

175. The Microbots are based on fire ants.

176. Stan Lee can be seen in a painting in one scene.

177. The "world" the animators created is bigger than the worlds of Tangled, Wreck-It Ralph and Frozen combined.

178. The villain is called Yokai. This means "phantom" in Japanese.

179. Honey Lemon is the only character that pronounces Hiro's name correctly.

180. Hans from Frozen and Flynn from Tangled can be seen on a Wanted sign in the police station.

181. The hardest thing to animate was Baymax's wings.

182. Stan Lee cameos in a post-credit scene.

183.   When Baymax tests his rocket, he blows up a statue of Hans from Frozen.

The Black Cauldron
1985

184.   This was the first Disney film to have no songs.

185.   The film was suspended from video release for years because it was considered too disturbing for children.

186.   This is considered to be the film that Disney is most ashamed of.

187.   Tim Burton was one of the crew members.

188.   This was the first Disney animated film that used computer technology.

Bolt
2008

189.   Bolt is an American White Shepherd.

190.   In Russia, the film is called Volt.

191.   In Poland, the film is called Lightning.

192.   In Bulgaria, the film is called Thunder.

193.   The Bolt tv show was supposed to be called The Omega Dog.

194.   Bolt's nemesis is Dr. Calico. A calico is a type of cat.

195.   The film's structure was heavily inspired by The Truman Show.

196.   Chloe Grace Moretz (who played Hit-Girl in Kick-Ass) performed all of her lines as Penny. Unfortunately, the studio didn't think her voice was right and she was replaced with Miley Cyrus.

Brave
2012

197. The short, La Luna, was shown in cinemas before this film.

198. The director was fired and replaced after two years. Another director continued making the film for another two years. Many people complained that the film has an uneven tone as if it has two stories slapped together.

199. Merida's name is Hebrew for "rebel."

200. This is the first PIXAR film where the lead is female.

201. The black bear is called Mor'du. It is based on the Gaelic term, "Mor Dubh," which means "large black one."

202. Reese Witherspoon was considered for Merida.

203. Merida is the first Disney princess which is not based on a pre-existing character or historical figure.

204.   Sean Connery was considered for King Fergus.

205.   Merida is the first Disney princess not to have a love interest.

206.   Merida is the first Disney princess of PIXAR.

207.   The original title was The Bear and the Bow.

208.   The DVD includes the short, The Legend of Mor'du.

Cars
2006

209.   The short, One Man Band, was shown in the cinemas before this film.

210.   The original title was Route 66.

211.   Lightning McQueen is based on Michael Jordan.

212.   This is the longest PIXAR film at 117 minutes.

213.   Fillmore says that the third blink of the stoplight in Radiator Springs is half a second slower. This is actually true.

214.   All of the jets in the sky make tyre marks.

215.   Guido's name is Italian for "I drive."

216.   Paul Newman thought this was his best performance in over twenty years.

217.   The Michael Schumacher Ferrari is actually voiced by Michael Schumacher.

218.   The original story was going to be about an electric car living in gas-consuming world.

219.   This is the final film of Paul Newman.

220.   The DVD includes a short called Mater and the Ghostlight.

Chicken Little
2005

221.   Chicken Little was supposed to be a girl.

222.   Chicken Little has 250,000 feathers.

223.   Jodie Foster was considered for Mallard.

224.   David Spade turned down the lead role.

225.   When Buck Cluck is driving Chicken Little to school, a bull can be seen in a China shop.

226.   Sigourney Weaver was the first choice for Mallard.

227.   Matthew Broderick was the first choice for Chicken Little.

228.   Jamie Lee Curtis auditioned for Mallard.

229.   Patrick Stewart plays Mr. Woolensworth. This is the first Disney film that Stewart has been a part of. He was offered nine other Disney roles in other films but he was always busy shooting Star Trek.

230. Madonna turned down the role of Mallard.

231. Martin Sheen was considered for Buck Cluck.

232. The first few minutes of the story is based on the fable, The Sky is Falling.

233. Michael J. Fox was considered for Chicken Little.

Chicken Run
2000

234.   Mel Gibson accepted the part of Rocky after his kids begged him to. They were huge fans of Wallace and Gromit, which was made by the same studio.

235.   3,370lbs of Plasticine was made for all of the chicken models.

236.   In Russia, the film is called Escape from the Hen House.

237.   Mrs. Tweedy's first name is Melisha. It is a reference to the word, "malicious."

238.   When Rocky leaves, Bunty says, "I don't even think he was American." This is a reference to the American actor, Mel Gibson, who is often mistaken as Australian.

Cinderella
1950

239.   This was the last Disney film released while Walt Disney was still alive.

240.   This was the first successful Disney film in seventeen years.

241.   The Prince is never called Prince Charming. In fact, his name is never given.

242.   The story takes place within twenty-four hours.

243.   In the original story, the lead character's name is Zezolla.

244.   Although Cinderella has orange hair in this film, she has blonde hair in the sequel.

245.   Ilene Woods plays Cinderella. As she got older, she suffered Alzheimer's disease and forgot that she was in this film.
    Nevertheless, she was always comforted by the song, A Dream Is A Wish Your Heart Makes.

246. Walt Disney said that the transformation of Cinderella's dress was the animation he was proudest of.

Coraline
2009

247.   This is the longest stop-motion film ever at 100 minutes.

248.   There's one scene where Coraline shows sixteen different expressions in thirty-five seconds. The animators said this was the hardest part of the film to animate.

249.   The film took over three years to make.

250.   Dawn French plays Miss Forcible and Jennifer Saunders plays Miss Spink. Originally, they were cast in opposing roles.

251.   It took up to four months and ten individuals to make one puppet of Coraline.

252.   One crew member knitted sweaters and other clothes for all of the characters.

253.   130 sets were built for the film.

Despicable Me
2010

254.   The Minions don't speak in gibberish. It is a language called "Minionese." Everything they say translates into actual words.

255.   The story of Sleeping Kittens is an actual book.

256.   The director does the voice of the Minions.

257.   Gru says that Miss Hattie's face is "como un burro." This is Spanish for "like a donkey."

258.   Steve Carell based his voice as Gru on Dracula and Khan from Star Trek.

259.   Gru's appearance is based on an Emperor penguin. This is fitting as the Emperor penguin is the only penguin where the male looks after the young.

260.   Mr. Perkins' design is based on The Boss from the comic strip and cartoon, Dilbert.

261.   Gru's first name is Felonius.

262. "Gru" is French for "crane."

263. The Minions were meant to look like normal henchmen but the studio didn't have enough money so their design was made simpler.

Despicable Me 2
2013

264.   Al Pacino recorded all of his lines for the villain but he had a disagreement with the director and dropped out. He was replaced with Benjamin Bratt.

265.   One of Gru's quick-dial buttons is for his Mom.

266.   Kristen Wiig plays Lucy. She played Miss Hattie in the first film.

267.   Javier Bardem was considered for the role of the main villain.

268.   When the ice cream truck appears, the Minions shout "gelato," which is Italian for "ice cream."

Dumbo
1941

269.   This is one of the only Disney animated features that is set in America.

270.   This was the first Disney film to be released on video cassette.

271.   Dumbo is friends with Timothy Mouse. In the original story, Timothy was a robin.

272.   Dumbo's mother is called Jumbo. The only thing she says in the film is Dumbo's name.

273.   This is John Lasseter's favourite film. He has directed five PIXAR films including Toy Story.

274.   During production, there was a huge animator strike going on. During the making of this film, half of the animators walked out. Their likeness was used for the clowns that "hit the big boss for a raise."

275.   This was the first Disney film to be set in modern day.

276.   Dumbo is the first protagonist in a
       Disney film to have no dialogue.

277.   Although many people find the crows to
       be offensive to African Americans, the studio
       pointed out that they are among the only
       friendly and intelligent characters in the
       film. Also, they were all voiced by black
       actors in a time where African-Americans
       struggled to get acting work.

278.   This was the film Walt Disney was
       proudest of.

The Emperor's New Groove
2000

279.   The original title was Kingdom of the Sun.

280.   Kuzco is named after the Inca capital, Cuzco.

281.   "Pacha" is Incan for "Earth."

282.   Yzma wears purple, a colour that is associated with royalty and madness.

283.   Some people assumed that the title is referencing Hans Christian Anderson's story, The Emperor's New Clothes. The two are not connected.

284.   In the diner, the saltshakers are shaped like llamas.

285.   Barbara Streisand was considered for Yzma.

286.   Renowned playwright, David Mamet, said the film's script was one of the most brilliantly innovative things Hollywood has produced in years.

287.   Pacha's wife, Chicha, is pregnant. This is the first Disney film to show a pregnant character.

Fantasia
1940

288. Mickey Mouse is the apprentice of the sorcerer, Yensid. The sorceror's name is "Disney" backwards.

289. Yensid's facial expressions are based on Walt Disney.

290. Yensid's appearance was used again for the King of Atlantis in the Disney film, Atlantis: The Lost Empire.

291. The original title was Colours and Music.

292. This is the longest Disney film ever at 125 minutes.

293. This is the first Disney feature film that Mickey Mouse appears in.

294. The beast in the final scene is not the Devil. It's a Slavic demon called Czernobog.

295. Bela Lugosi modelled for the demon, Czernobog. Bela Lugosi is famous for playing Dracula.

296.   Disney still get complaints that the final scene is too scary.

Finding Nemo
2003

297.   PIXAR made the water look so realistic that they actually had to make it look LESS realistic in case audience members thought it was real footage of the ocean.

298.   The director, Andrew Stanton, does the voice of Crush the turtle.

299.   200 turtles were animated for Crush's scene.

300.   Ellen DeGeneres got cast as Dory after the PIXAR studio watched her on her show and noticed that she changed the subject every five seconds.

301.   Dory keeps getting Nemo's name wrong. She calls him Chico, Elmo, Harpo, Bingo and Fabio.

302.   The great white shark is called Bruce. Bruce is the name of the shark in Jaws. It was named after the director's lawyer.

303.   Marlin was originally voiced by William H. Macy. Although Macy recorded all of his

lines, PIXAR felt that his voice didn't suit Marlin and he was replaced with Albert Brooks.

304. Dory is a Regal Blue Tang fish.

305. Nemo's name is a reference to Captain Nemo in Jules Verne's novel, 20,000 Leagues Under the Sea. It means "nobody" in Latin.

306. The director pitched the idea to PIXAR in an hour-long presentation. When he finished, the head of PIXAR said, "You had me at fish."

Flushed Away
2006

307.   This was made by Aardman studios, the same studio that makes the Wallace and Gromit animations.

308.   This was the first CGI-film that Aardman made.

309.   Aardman said that the most difficult thing to use stop-motion effects on is water. Since this story is based in a sewer, he thought it would be impossible to do with stop-motion and agreed to use CGI.

310.   In one scene, Hugh Jackman's character, Roddy, pulls out a Wolverine outfit from a wardrobe. Hugh Jackman portrays Wolverine in the X-Men films.

311.   At the start of the film, one of the outfits Roddy pulls out of the wardrobe belongs to Wallace from Wallace and Gromit.

312.   Nicole Kidman was considered for the role of Rita.

313.   William Shatner auditioned for a role.

314.   In Tabitha's room, Alex the Lion can be seen from Madagascar as a toy.

315.   One of the frozen rats in the fridge is Hans Solo from Star Wars.

316.   Johnny Depp was considered for Le Frog.

317.   One of Tabitha's toys is Gromit.

318.   A picture of Shrek appears on the fridge.

319.   When Roddy gets flushed, an orange fish shouts, "Have you seen my dad?" This is a reference to Finding Nemo.

320.   The Toad wears a Freemason ring.

321.   Kevin Kline auditioned for Le Frog.

322.   Robert De Niro auditioned for Spike. The part went to Andy Serkis.

The Fox and the Hound
1981

323.   The fox is called Tod. Tod is derived from the Middle English word "todde" which means "fox."

324.   The film was delayed for a year as many animators left to join Disney's competitor, Don Bluth. Bluth made The Secret of NIMH, American Tail, and The Land Before Time.

325.   This is the tenth Disney film that Kurt Russell has acted in.

326.   The bear's roar is the same as Shere Kahn's roar in The Jungle Book.

Frankenweenie
2012

327.   The turtle is called Shelley. This is an obvious reference to the fact that turtles have shells. It is also a reference to Mary Shelley, the writer of Frankenstein, which was the main inspiration of this film.

328.   The mayor is called Burgermeister, which means "mayor" in German.

329.   Victor's neighbour is called Elsa Van Helsing. Van Helsing battled Dracula in Bram Stoker's novel, Dracula.

330.   Elsa is named after Elsa Lanchester who played the Bride in the Bride of Frankenstein.

331.   This film is a remake of the thirty-minute short that Tim Burton made in 1984.

332.   Edgar Gore's name is a reference to Ygor, a character in the Son of Frankenstein.

333.   Shelley the tortoise becomes a gigantic monster. This is a reference to the film,

Gamera, which is about colossal tortoise-like creature.

334.   Burton made the 1984 version of Frankenweenie when he worked for Disney. Disney considered the film to be too scary for children. As a result, Burton was fired.

335.   Elsa's dog is called Persephone. Persephone was the wife of Hades, lord of the underworld in Greek mythology.

336.   Persephone has a white streak in her hair, just like the Bride in Bride of Frankenstein.

Frozen
2013

337.   The short, Get a Horse!, was shown in the cinema before this film.

338.   Elsa is twenty-one. Anna is eighteen.

339.   The film is based on Hans Christian Anderson's story, The Snow Queen.

340.   Hans Christian Anderson's name is referenced with four of the character's names – Hans, Kristoff, Anna and Sven.

341.   Elsa was supposed to turn into the villain when she fled from the village. But after executives heard the song, Let It Go, (you may have heard of it,) they changed their mind.

342.   This is the only animated film to make over a billion dollars.

343.   This is, by far, the most successful animated film ever. It made $1,276,480,335.

344.   This is the eight most successful film ever.

345.   Elsa is the only Disney princess that is not a teenager.

346.   Rapunzel and Flynn can be seen briefly in the beginning when the games open during the "For the First Time in Forever" song.

347.   Elsa is the second Disney princess to become a Queen. The first was Kida in Atlantis: The Lost Empire.

348.   The film has a post-credits scene.

349.   Jack Whitehall voiced one of the trolls but his dialogue was cut.

350.   Idina Menzel plays Elsa. This is the third time she has collaborated with Disney. She played the sorceress, Circe, in the Hercules tv series and she played Nancy in the film, Enchanted.

351.   Han's horse is called Sitron. "Sitron" is Norwegian for "lemon."

352.   Idina Menzel's son bragged that her mum sings the song, Let It Go. When he said

this in school, one kid said, "So does everyone else."

353.   Three million hours went into making this film over 2.5 years.

354.   The colours in Elsa's ice castle represent her feelings – blue is happy, red is fear and yellow is anger.

355.   When the snow monster screams, its gesture and facial expression is identical to when Sully from Monsters, Inc. screams.

356.   Olaf's name is a reference to "Oh laugh."

357.   The first and last thing that the King says is, "Elsa."

358.   Jennifer Lee is the director. This was her directorial debut.

359.   Elsa and Kristoff never speak to each other.

360.   A psychotherapist called Dr. Jill Squyres concluded that Elsa has Borderline Personality Disorder.

361.   It took nine months to animate Elsa's castle.

362.   Anna's horse is called Kjekk. It means "handsome" in Norwegian.

363.   Anna is the only Disney princess to perform a duet with the villain.

364.   In most films, good characters wear bright colours and villains wear dark colours. But in this film, the villain wears the brightest clothing.

365.   The village of Arendelle was inspired by the towns of Norway.

366.   Anna does a chicken dance when she's dancing with the Duke. It is the exact same chicken dance that Lindsay Bluth does in the tv show, Arrested Development.

367.   The giant snowman that Elsa creates is called Marshmallow.

Gnomeo & Juliet
2011

368. The Terrafirminator lawnmower is voiced by Hulk Hogan. (That is a sentence I never thought I would write.)

369. In the Terrafirminator ad, the fine print reads –

i) Not recommended for residential use
ii) Not recommended for commercial use either
iii) Do not use vehicle while sleeping
iv) Not recommended for children under 3
v) Or 4
vi) After use, lawn may appear completely destroyed
vii) Do not be alarmed – this is perfectly normal
viii) Side effects may include persistent feelings of awesomeness
ix) In rare instances, some people may explode when viewing the Terrafirminator
x) Maker of the Terrafirminator will not be held responsible for infidelity caused by the use of this product.

370. Ewan McGregor was considered for Gnomeo.

371. Kate Winslet was considered for Juliet.

372. The story takes place in Stratford-Upon-Avon, the birthplace of William Shakespeare. It is here where he wrote Romeo & Juliet.

373. The moving company is called As U Like It. This is a reference to the Shakespeare play, As You Like It.

374. Two houses numbers can be seen which say "2B" and "Not 2B."

375. The glue that the Gnomes use is called The Taming of the Glue. This is a reference to the play, The Taming of the Shrew.

376. One of the trucks is from a company called Tempest Teapot. This is a reference to the Shakespeare play, The Tempest.

377. One of the trucks reads Rosencrantz and Guildenstern moving company. Rosencrantz and Guildenstern were two characters from the play, Hamlet.

The Good Dinosaur
2015

378.   The short, Sanjay's Super Team, was
shown in the cinema before this film.

379.   This film was released a few months
after Inside Out. This is the first time that
PIXAR released two films in the same year.

380.   The film was supposed to be released on
May 30th, 2014. It was released on
November 25th, 2015.

381.   This film took six years to make.

382.   This film had more production problems
than any other film in PIXAR history. Many
people were fired or replaced including the
director, crew and several actors.

383.   Eighty PIXAR workers were fired in
2012, while this film was in production. One
year later, another sixty-seven people were
fired.

384.   In the original script, the main character,
Arlo, was going to be seventeen.

The Great Mouse Detective
1986

385. Rattigan's painting smiles any time he references it.

386. Rattigan was played by Vincent Price. Rattigan's physicality was based directly on Price.

387. John Cleese was the first choice for the lead, Basil.

388. Michael Palin was considered for a role.

389. Most animations take three or four years to make. This film only took one year to make.

390. The original title was Basil of Baker Street.

391. A toy of Dumbo can be seen in the toy shop.

Happy Feet
2006

392.   Robin Williams, Huge Jackman, Nicole
Kidman and Brittany Murphy performed all
of their own singing.

393.   All of the dancers in the film had to go to
Penguin School so they could move like a
penguin.

394.   The male penguins have an orange spot
on their beaks. The females have a pink spot.

395.   Mumble's dancing is based on Fred
Astaire.

396.   The film's code name was Cats Don't
Dance.

397.   This was Steve Irwin's final film. The
movie is dedicated to him.

Hercules
2000

398.　James Woods plays Hades. He said he played the character like a sleazy car salesman.

399.　James Woods said that Hades is the best character he has ever played. He loves the character so much that he is more than happy to play him for any television show or video game.

400.　When Hercules enters Phil's hut, he bangs his head off the Argo mast. In Greek mythology, Jason died when the mast hit his head.

401.　In this story, Hercules' mother is Hera. In Greek myth, Hercules' mother was a mortal woman called Alcmene.

402.　Pegasus is created out of clouds. In Greek myth, he was created from Medusa's blood.

403.　When the kids are trapped under the boulder, one of them shouts, "Someone call IXII." These are the Roman numerals for 911.

404.   The Spice Girls were considered for the Muses.

405.   There are five Muses in the film. In Greek myth, there were nine. The five Muses in this film are called Calliope, Clio, Thalia, Terpsichore and Melpomene.

406.   John Lithgow was cast as Hades and recorded all of his dialogue but he was eventually replaced by James Woods.

407.   John Goodman was considered for Zeus.

Horton Hears a Who!
2008

408.   This is the second Dr. Seuss adaption that Jim Carrey has been a part of. The first was How the Grinch Stole Christmas.

409.   This is the first Dr. Seuss adaptation to be fully animated by CGI.

410.   Green eggs can be seen at the Mayor's breakfast table. This is a reference to the Dr. Seuss story, Green Eggs and Ham.

411.   Dr. Seuss said that this story was an allegory to how Hiroshima and Nagasaki were destroyed in World War II but nobody seemed to care because the cities were far away and couldn't be seen.

412.   The Grinch cameos as a snowman.

413.   The film was shipped to cinemas under the fake title, 88 Keys.

414.   The first painting that the Mayor shows Jo-Jo is of the writer, Theodore Geisel (Dr. Seuss.)

How to Train Your Dragon
2010

415.   Toothless' movements and facial expressions are based on a horse and a kitten.

416.   The sounds that Toothless makes are based on an elephant seal.

417.   Gobber has fourteen hand attachments.

418.   Hiccup is the only character to call Toothless by name.

419.   Hiccup is the first teenage lead in a DreamWorks film.

420.   David Tennant cameos as Spitelout.

421.   Hiccup is fifteen years old.

422.   Stoic is 7ft 2.

423.   Hiccup is the only character in the story that is left-handed; another example that shows he's different from everyone else.

424. At the end of the film, all of the Vikings hold their swords in their left hand to show that they support Hiccup.

How to Train Your Dragon 2
2014

425.   Most of the story was meant to be saved for the third film. The director decided he shouldn't "save ideas" for a film because it would compromise the story's potential.

426.   Valka was originally going to be the villain.

427.   Gobber is the first gay character in a DreamWorks film.

The Hunchback of Notre Dame
1996

428. Ian McKellen was considered for the villain, Frollo.

429. The heretic is Jafar in his Old Man disguise from Aladdin.

430. Belle from Beauty and the Beast can be seen in a crowd sequence.

431. Frollo's horse is called Snowball.

432. Kevin Kline plays Phoebus. It was his idea to call his horse Achilles because he thought it would be funny to say, "Achilles, heel."

433. Two of the gargoyles are called Victor and Hugo. Victor Hugo is the author of the novel, The Hunchback of Notre Dame.

434. This is Michael Eisner's favourite film. He is the CEO of Disney.

Ice Age
2002

435.   At the test screening, the children burst into tears when Diego died so the ending was redone so he survived.

436.   Although Scrat is supposed to be a fictional creature, a prehistoric animal was discovered in 2009 that looks exactly like him. This creature is called a Cronopio.

437.   The cave drawings are exact duplicates of the first cave drawings ever found.

438.   Ving Rhames was considered for the role of Manny.

439.   Pre-production took over a year before anything was animated.

The Incredibles
2004

440.   The short, Boundin', was shown in the cinema before this film.

441.   In the beginning of the film, Mr. Incredible says, "Fly home, Buddy. I work alone." to IncrediBoy. When Syndrome flashes back to this moment, it doesn't match up the way the scene was shown before. Originally, the villain, Bomb Voyage, was in the background but in Syndrome's memory, Bomb Voyage is nowhere to be seen. This is to show that Syndrome is remembering the moment incorrectly, proving that his mind has become unhinged and he has become completely obsessed with Mr. Incredible.

442.   Brad Bird is the director. He came up with the idea for The Incredibles from his own experience of trying to balance a career with his family.

443.   The film was nearly called The Invincibles.

444.   The film's codename was Tights.

445.   Some critics complained that the dynamic of the Incredibles was too similar to The Simpsons. That's probably because Brad Bird was the Story Consultant for The Simpsons for years. In his own words, "It was my job to make jokes funny."

446.   Animators find human clothing extremely difficult to animate. As a result, a tailor had to come into PIXAR studio and explain how every type of clothing should look and why.

447.   Syndrome uses a weapon called Zero Point Energy. Astrophysicist, Stephen Hawking, believes that this concept exists (but he calls it the Casimir Effect.)

448.   Mr. Incredible lives in Metroville.

449.   Brad Bird wanted the film to be cel-shaded. The animation during the end credits shows how the film was supposed to look.

450.   All of the Incredibles powers are identical to the Marvel superheroes, the Fantastic Four – Mr. Fantastic, Invisible Girl, Human Torch and the Thing.

Mr. Incredible is superstrong like the Thing.
Elastigirl can superstretch like Mr. Fantastic.
Violet can turn invisible and create
forcefields like Invisible Girl.
Dash can move at superspeed like the
Human Torch.

451.   Joaquin Phoenix was considered for the
role of Syndrome.

452.   The DVD came with a short called Jack-
Jack Attack.

453.   The DVD has a terrible cartoon that
shows the adventures of Mr. Incredible and
Frozone. The cartoon also has an audio
commentary with the two characters. Most
of the commentary involves Frozone
complaining that the cartoon changed his
skin tone. He says things like, "I'm white?
They made me a white guy?!" Mr. Incredible
tries to calm him down by saying, "Well...
maybe the prints faded."

Inside Out
2015

454.   The short, Lava, was shown in the
cinema before this film.

455.   Some Emotions were scrapped including
Surprise, Pride and Trust.

456.   Riley's clothes get darker as the film
progresses.

457.   The newspaper article that Anger reads
always relates to what's happening to Riley.

458.   Riley's father daydreams about football.
In some countries, this daydream was
changed to ice hockey.

459.   Nemo appears on a board game called
Find Me when Joy and Sadness are in
Imagination Land.

460.   In Riley's classroom, a map with pins on
it can be seen in the back of the room. Each
pin represents where each of the PIXAR
films are based.

461. Despite the film's complexity, it was made by forty-five animators. That's half the animators PIXAR had on their other films.

462. Riley's chief emotion is Joy. Her mother's is Sadness and her father's is Anger.

463. Some of the memory balls in Riley's minds contain scenes from other PIXAR films.

464. The DVD includes the short, Riley's First Date.

The Iron Giant
1999

465.   The Iron Giant is voiced by Vin Diesel. It was one of his first roles.

466.   The Giant only says fifty-three words.

467.   Peter Cullen was considered for the Giant. He is most famous for playing Optimus Prime in the Transformers franchise.

468.   The director cast Vin Diesel as the Giant because he reminded him of the character himself; Diesel looks extremely muscular and dangerous but spoke in a relaxing and soothing voice.

469.   Hogarth's surname is Hughes. This is an homage to Ted Hughes, the writer of the original story, The Iron Man.

470.   There was an extra scene that showed the Iron Giant's dreams appearing on a television set that showed his race destroying a planet. This was removed as it was considered too disturbing. A rough draft of it can be seen on the DVD.

471.   The tentacles that come out of the Giant's back are modelled off the spaceships in The War of the Worlds.

472.   The Superman comic that Hogarth shows to the Giant is Action Comics #188 from 1954.

473.   The story was supposed to be a musical.

The Jungle Book
1967

474.   Walt Disney died before the film was released. It was believed that if this film failed, Disney would stop releasing animated films. Luckily, The Jungle Book was a huge success.

475.   The Vultures were supposed to be voiced by The Beatles.

476.   The film was nearly called A Boy, A Bear and A Black Cat.

477.   Elvis was considered for a role.

478.   The most difficult thing to animate was Shere Kahn's stripes.

479.   Most people mispronounce Mowgli's name. It's pronounced "MAU-glee." This was confirmed by the writer's daughter, Elsie. She never forgave Disney for this mistake.

480.   In the Rudyard Kipling novel, Kaa is a helpful and friendly snake.

481.   Kaa's song, Trust in Me, was written for Mary Poppins.

482.   The character's names are Hindi for their species.
"Baloo" means "bear."
"Hathi" means "elephant."
"Bagheera" means "panther."
"Shere Kahn" means "Tiger King."

483.   All of the characters' movements are based on the actors who provided their voices.

484.   This was the first Disney animated feature to show the credits of the actors in the opening.

485.   Bruce Reitherman performed the voice of Mowgli. He now makes documentaries about wild life.

Kung Fu Panda
2008

486.   Jackie Chan did all of voice over work in five hours. In this session, he did his dialogue in English, Mandarin and Cantonese.

487.   Each of the Furious Five's fighting style is based on their species – tiger, mantis, crane, monkey and viper.

488.   The prison is called Chor Ghom Prison. This is Cantonese for "sit in prison."

489.   "Oogway" is Chinese for "Tortoise."

490.   "Shifu" is Chinese for "teacher-master."

491.   The animators said that Kung Fu Hustle was a massive influence on this film.

492.   The film's code name was Daydreamer.

493.   Po's fighting style is Bear.

Kung Fu Panda 2
2011

494.   This is the first animated film that Jean Claude Van Damme has performed in. It is also the first time he has done voiceover work.

495.   Shen's fighting style is called Cai Li Fo. This technique involves fighting with a metal fan. Instead of a fan, Shen uses his feathers.

496.   The original title was going to be Pandamoneum.

497.   Another potential title was going to be The Kaboom of Doom.

498.   Jean Claude Van Damme voices Croc. Croc does the splits in one scene. This is a signature move for Van Damme.

Lady and the Tramp
1955

499.   At the time, this was the most successful Disney cartoon since Snow White and the Seven Dwarves.

500.   Human faces are rarely seen. This was done intentionally to maintain a dog's perspective.

501.   The setting was partly inspired by Disney's hometown, Marceline in Missouri.

502.   A dream sequence that shows dogs walking humans was scrapped after it received negative feedback.

503.   The trailer spoiled the ending.

504.   This is one of the few Disney films where there is no villain.

505.   Walt Disney hated the spaghetti-eating scene. It is now one of the most iconic moments in Disney history.

The Land Before Time
1988

506.   This film has thirteen sequels.

507.   Of the fourteen films, this is the only one that isn't a musical.

508.   This film contains twenty-nine dinosaurs.

509.   Five dinosaurs in this film were already extinct at the time that this story takes place.

510.   George Lucas and Steven Spielberg produced the film.

511.   Spielberg and Lucas wanted the film to have no dialogue.

512.   Ten minutes of the film was lost and has never been found.

513.   Nineteen scenes were cut or heavily trimmed as they were considered too scary.

514.   Littlefoot is an Apatosaurus, Spike is a Stegosaurus, Petrie is a Pteranodon and Ducky is a Parasaurolophus. Cera is

supposed to be a Triceratops but she is actually a Torosaurus.

515.   Cera was supposed to be male called Bambo.

516.   Littlefoot was originally going to be called Thunderfoot.

The Lego Movie
2014

517.   The word "Lego" is never said at any point in the film.

518.   The wizard is called Vitruvius. He is named after the Roman architect, who lived in 100 B.C. His name means "Master Builder."

519.   Vitruvius' staff is a chewed-up lollipop.

520.   This is the first animated film for Morgan Freeman.

521.   To make the Lego look more realistic, the blocks are covered in scratches, fades and fingerprints.

522.   The animators never "cheated" with the Lego blocks. Everything designed in the film would look exactly the same way if it was made of Lego.

523.   Batman throws fifteen Batarangs at the red button in the "First try" scene.

524. Morgan Freeman has starred in every film of the Dark Knight trilogy. This means that this is the fourth film he has been in with Batman.

525. Freeman said that Will Arnett's depiction of Batman is the best performance of the character.

526. MetalBeard's Five Laws of the Sea are -
i)   Never place your rear end on a pirate's face.
ii)   Never release a Kraken.
iii) Never put ye hand in a clam's mouth.
iv)   Always abandon a lost cause.
v)   Never wear a dress on Tuesday.

527. Vitruvius is wearing a tie-dye shirt and blue jeans under his robe.

528. This is the first film to feature Wonder Woman.

529. Robert Downey Jr. was considered for Emmett.

530. Emma Stone was considered for Wyldstyle.

Lilo & Stitch
2002

531. "Lilo" means "generous one."

532. Tia Carrere (from True Lies and Wayne's World) and Jason Scott Lee (who played Mowgli in the 1994 film, The Jungle Book) helped the writers with the Hawaiian dialogue and accents.

533. Two of the aliens are based on Piglet and Tigger.

534. Stitch doesn't have pupils. This made it very difficult to show what emotion Stitch is feeling since he can barely talk. Instead of adding in pupils, the animators became more creative with his gestures.

535. A sign above Lilo's door says "Kapu." This is Hawaiian for "Keep Out."

The Lion King
1994

536.　This film was made by the Disney Team B. This was supposed to be the "filler" Disney film while the "superior" Team A was making Pocahontas. Disney thought Pocahontas was going to be a success and The Lion King was going to fail. The Lion King is considered to be the greatest Disney film ever.

537.　Although it is common knowledge that the film is heavily inspired by William Shakespeare's play, Hamlet, it is also based on the Ancient Egyptian story of Osiris. Osiris was killed by his evil brother, Seth. Osiris' son, Horus, exiles himself until his father's ghost beckons him to return and exact revenge on Seth.

538.　The story is very similar to a Niger Congo tale about a king called Sundiata, (which means "lion king,") who was banished from his home by his family after his father died. He eventually returns and battles the evil wizard king who has taken over his former home.

539.   Another story the film resembles is Kimba the White Lion. The stories are so similar that Matthew Broderick thought The Lion King was a remake when he was cast as Simba.

540.   The translation of The Circle of Life is, "Here comes a lion, Father/ Oh, yes, it's a lion / Here comes a lion, / Oh yes, it's a lion / A lion We're going to conquer / A lion A lion and a leopard come to this open place."

541.   The song Rafiki sings translates into, "Thank you very much, squash banana, you're a baboon and I'm not."

542.   In the original draft, Scar was simply an evil lion and wasn't related to Mufasa.

543.   The hyena march during the Be Prepared song was recreated by watching footage of Nazis goose-stepping.

544.   In the film, lions are graceful, powerful animals and hyenas are mindless scavengers. Ironically, it is almost the opposite in real life. Hyenas are ferocious and very intelligent. Lions, on the other hand, scavenge the animals that hyenas kill.

545.   This was the last film supervised by Jeffrey Katzenberg before he created Disney's competitor, DreamWorks.

546.   Most of the characters' name are Swahili words. Simba means "lion."

547.   Simba's mother is called Sarabi. Her name means "mirage."

548.   Simba's mentor is called Rafiki. His name means "friend."

549.   Pumbaa means "simpleton."

550.   The leader of the hyenas is called Shenzi. Her name means "barbarian."

551.   Shenzi's lackey is called Banzai. His name means "skulk."

552.   One of the bugs that Timon picks up has Mickey Mouse ears.

553.   Scar's claws are never retracted at any point.

554.   The stampede scene took three years to animate.

555.   Scar's face is based on Jeremy Irons' face.

556.   Originally, the main villain was a jackal.

557.   Sean Connery wanted to play Mufasa.

558.   When Mufasa tells Simba about the Great Kings of the Past, one of the star alignments is of Mickey Mouse.

559.   This was the most successful film of 1994.

560.   This was the first Disney cartoon to be dubbed into Zulu.

561.   This was the most successful animated film ever until Frozen.

562.   When Mufasa and Simba talk about the stars, the constellation for Leo (lion) is clearly visible.

563.   Simba's mane was inspired by Jon Bon Jovi's hair.

564.   None of the lion roars were from actual lions. Frank Welker provided all of the lion roars himself. Welker is best known for providing the voice of Megatron in the animated series, Transformers.

565.   During the song, Be Prepared, Jeremy Irons roars, "You won't get a sniff without me!" He strained his throat so much when he said that line that he lost his voice and couldn't continue the song. The rest of the song is voiced by Jim Cummings who sings in Jeremy Irons voice perfectly. The transition is so seamless, it's impossible to notice.

The Little Mermaid
1989

566.   This was Disney's first fairy tale in thirty years. The last one was Sleeping Beauty in 1959.

567.   Prince Eric was played by Christopher Barnes. He was only sixteen when he recorded his voice.

568.   In the opening scene with King Triton, Mickey Mouse, Goofy, Donald Duck and Kermit the Frog can be seen in the crowd.

569.   In Greek mythology, Poseidon was the God of the sea. In this film, the God of the Sea is Poseidon's son, Triton.

570.   Ursula is a Cecaelia – half-human, half-octopus.

571.   Ariel's sisters are called Attina, Alana, Aquata, Arista, Adella and Andrina.

572.   The tails of the seven daughters of Triton correspond with the colours of the rainbow – red, orange, yellow, green, blue, indigo and violet.

573.   Patrick Stewart was supposed to play Triton.

574.   Jim Carrey auditioned for Eric.

575.   Michael Richards (Kramer from Seinfeld) was considered for Scuttle the seagull.

576.   Matthew Broderick was considered for Eric. He would go on to voice Simba in The Lion King.

577.   Ariel is the first Disney Princess to have red hair. She is also the first Disney Princess to have siblings.

Madagascar
2005

578.   Julien was only supposed to have two lines. After Sacha Baron Cohen was cast in the role, he improvised so much dialogue that he became a fundamental part of the entire series.

579.   The film begins with a lion, zebra, giraffe and a hippo in Central Park Zoo. In real life, none of these animals are in this zoo.

580.   Madonna was considered for Gloria the hippo.

581.   Melman the giraffe wears tissue boxes on his feet. This is a reference to Howard Hughes who did the same thing due to his severe hypochondria.

Madagascar: Escape 2 Africa
2008

582.   Ben Stiller plays Alex. Young Alex is played by Ben's son, Quinn.

583.   Jada Pinkett Smith plays Gloria. Young Gloria is played by her daughter, Willow.

584.   Bernie Mac played Zuba. This film was dedicated to him as he died before the film was released.

585.   The original title was The Crate Escape.

586.   All of the zebras are voiced by Chris Rock.

587.   The mark on Alex's paw is shaped like Africa. It even includes the island of Madagascar.

Megamind
2010

588.   The film's plot was based on the premise, "What if Lex Luthor defeated Superman?"

589.   Megamind's posters say, "No you can't." This is an obvious reference to Barack Obama's slogan, "Yes we can."

590.   Ben Stiller was considered for the lead.

591.   Megamind's lackey, Minion, is based on the alien in the film, Robot Monster.

592.   The original title was Mastermind.

593.   Robert Downey Jr. was the first choice for Megamind.

594.   Guillermo del Toro edited some of the film. Del Toro is best known for directing Pacific Rim and Pan's Labyrinth.

595.   Megamind mispronounces twenty words throughout the film.

596.   Metro City is located in Michigan.

Minions
2015

597.   The director voiced all 899 Minions.

598.   The Minion language is a mix of Hebrew, English, Spanish, German, French, Italian, Indonesian, Portuguese and Malay.

599.   This is the first film where Sandra Bullock plays a villain.

600.   The Minions sometimes speak in perfect Indonesian. They say "terima kasih," which means "thank you," "kemari," which means "come here" and "yang mulia," which means "your highness."

601.   One of the Minions usually says "sepala." Although this sounds like gibberish, he is actually saying "It's that way" in French. He always says this in the right context.

602.   A young Gru can be seen at the VillainCon. He is watching Dr. Nefario using his freeze ray gun.

603.   The villain from The Smurfs, Gargamel, is in front of the Minions at VillianCon.

Monsters, Inc.
2001

604.   The short, For the Birds, was shown in the cinema before this film.

605.   Mary Gibbs was only two-and-a-half when she played Boo. PIXAR struggled getting Mary Gibbs to record her lines so they just followed her with a microphone. Whatever she said became her lines in the film.

606.   Nemo appears as a teddy in Boo's room. Finding Nemo didn't come out for two years.

607.   Sulley was made of 2,320,413 hairs.

608.   Hair is the most difficult thing to animate. PIXAR created the furry character, Sulley, to challenge themselves.

609.   It was John Goodman's idea to have Steve Buscemi cast as the villain, Randall.

610.   The sushi restaurant is called Harryhausen's. It is named after Ray Harryhausen, a special effects designer who

created many classic movie monsters like the Cyclops, Medusa, the Kraken, etc.

611.   Sulley's chair has a hole to let his tail through.

612.   This was the first PIXAR film where each character was designed by a different animator. This was done so each character would look as different as possible.

613.   Bill Murray was offered the part of Sulley.

614.   The DVD comes with a short called Mike's New Car.

615.   Boo's real name is Mary.

Monster's University
2013

616.   The short, Blue Umbrella, was shown in the cinema before this film.

617.   This was PIXAR's first prequel.

618.   Kelsey Grammar was considered for a role.

619.   Monsters Inc.'s lead competitors are Fear Co. and Scream Ind.

620.   In the first trailer, the slug monster "running" to class had buck teeth. In the finished film, he didn't.

621.   Ariel's line from The Little Mermaid, "No Daddy, I love him!" can be heard during the Don't Scare the Teen scene.

622.   In the original script, Mike and Sully get trapped in the human world.

623.   Although Helen Mirren was offered the role of Dean Hardscrabble, she insisted that she should audition to make sure she was the right choice.

Mulan
1998

624.   Jackie Chan voices Shang in the Chinese version.

625.   Mulan is left-handed. This is a common trait in Disney characters.

626.   Tia Carrere was considered for the lead role. Carrere is best known for playing Cassandra in Wayne's World and Juno in True Lies.

627.   The film was nearly rated PG because of the use of the word, "cross-dresser."

628.   Bruce Willis was considered for Li Shang.

629.   This film is credited for launching Christina Aguilera's career since her song, Reflection, was in the film.

630.   Chi Fu's name is Chinese for "bully."

631.   Mulan's name means "magnolia."

632.   This was the first Disney film on DVD.

Over the Hedge
2006

633. Bill Murray was the first choice for RJ.

634. Bruce Willis replaced Jim Carrey at the last minute.

635. 237 people worked on this film.

636. This is the only DreamWorks film that is based on a comic strip.

637. The forest part of the hedge is based on the hedge in front of the DreamWorks building.

638. Gene Wilder turned down a role.

The Peanuts Movie
2015

639.   The short, Cosmic Scrat-tastophy, was shown in cinemas before this film.

640.   This is the first Peanuts film in thirty-five years.

641.   Charlie Brown isn't bald. He has very faded blond hair.

642.   This is the first Peanuts film since the death of its creator, Charles M. Schulz, in 2000.

643.   The trees never sway in the film. This was emulating the same look as the original comic strip.

644.   The comic strip was supposed to be called L'il Folks.

645.   It took nine years to make this film.

646.   The film was released fifty years after A Charlie Brown Christmas, which is considered to be the best Peanuts cartoon.

647.   The film was released sixty-five years after the first Peanuts comic strip.

648.   Charlie Brown's book report is on War and Peace. This was the writer's favourite novel.

Peter Pan
1953

649.   This story is based on J.M. Barrie's play. It was the first story to feature the name, "Wendy."

650.   Walt Disney played Peter Pan in a play.

651.   This is Michael Jackson's favourite film.

652.   Walt Disney was trying to buy the rights for this story since 1935.

653.   Walt Disney was disappointed with this film because he found Peter Pan cold and unlikeable. Experts on the original story said that Pan was portrayed perfectly as he was originally written as a selfish and ruthless.

Pinocchio
1940

654.   A scene was cut that showed Geppetto telling Pinocchio of his grandfather, who was a pine tree.

655.   Honest John's real name is John Worthington Foulfellow.

656.   The original budget was $500,000. It ballooned to $2.5 million.

657.   When Pinocchio is a wooden boy, he has three fingers. When he turns into a real boy, he has four.

658.   In the original story, Jiminy Cricket is called The Talking Cricket.

659.   The film was in production for nine months before Walt Disney inserted Jiminy Cricket into the story.

660.   Walt Disney shut down production at one point to rethink the story and redesign some of the characters.

661.   The film wasn't released in Germany or Japan until the 1950s because of the war.

662.   The film flopped because it came out during World War II and very few people were going to the cinema.

663.   Some people think Pinocchio dies in the sea because he drowned but this is impossible since he doesn't have lungs. He died because he smashed into the rocks.

664.   Figaro the cat is Walt Disney's favourite character in the film.

Pocahontas
1995

665.   Only two Disney films are based on a true story; this and Mulan.

666.   The tree, Grandmother Willow, was originally going to be a male called Old Man River.

667.   The film was in production for five years.

668.   Christian Bale has been in two different Pocahontas films. He plays Thomas in this film and he plays Rolfe in the 2005 film, The New World.

669.   All of the animals were going to talk but this idea was abandoned to make the subject matter more serious.

670.   In real life, Pocahontas was called Matoaka. Her people nicknamed her "Pocahontas" which means "frisky." She was given the name because she willingly interacted with the settlers. The term "Pocahontas" was considered an extremely insulting term among her people.

671.   In real life, Pocahontas was only thirteen when the settlers came to her land.

672.   John Candy was cast as Redfeather the turkey. Although he had most of his voiceover work done, the character was scrapped when Candy suddenly died.

673.   It took fifty-five animators to design Pocahontas.

674.   Jeffrey Katzenberg was the studio head of Disney at the time of this film's release. He was so proud of it that he thought it would be Oscar nominated for Best Film. The film was universally panned and it made very little money.

675.   Pocahontas is American. The only other American Disney princess is Tiana from the 2009 film, The Princess and the Frog.

676.   Sean Bean was considered for John Smith.

The Prince of Egypt
1998

677.   Val Kilmer does the voice of God and
Moses. This is a reference to the film, The
Ten Commandments, where Charlton Heston
voices Moses and God.

678.   In the Bible, Aaron turns the staff into a
snake, not Moses.

679.   Steven Martin, Ralph Fiennes, Michelle
Pfeiffer and Martin Short performed their
own singing.

680.   Ofra Haza played Yocheved. Of the
twenty languages the film was dubbed in,
Haza dubbed seventeen of them herself.

681.   At the time, this was the most expensive
animated film ever at $70 million.

682.   This was co-directed by Brenda
Chapman. She also co-directed the film,
Brave.

683.   A shadow can be seen in the Red Sea
after it has risen. Many viewers assume the
shadow is of a whale. It is actually of a

Megalodon shark, the largest shark to ever exist.

684. This film was banned in Malaysia and Indonesia.

685. The film takes place in 1,200 BC.

686. The Red Sea parting scene required ten animators and took two years to animate.

The Princess and the Frog
2009

687. The original title was The Frog Princess.

688. Tiana is left-handed.

689. Tiana was originally called Maddy.

690. Beyoncé was considered for Tiana.

691. Dr. Facilier's face is based on the Voodoo god of magic.

692. The prince is called Naveen. "Naveen" is Indian for "new."

693. Dr. Facilier's teeth are based on Keith David, the actor who provided the voice for the character.

694. Jennifer Hudson auditioned for a part.

695. Facilier is Disney's first black villain.

696. This was the first 2D Disney film where all of the voice actors do their own singing since Beauty and the Beast.

Ratatouille
2007

697.   The short, Lifted, was shown before this film in the cinema.

698.   The dog that barks at Remy when he climbs out of the sewer for the first time is Dug from the film, Up.

699.   To save time and money, no human characters have toes.

700.   Hair is the hardest thing to animate so Remy was exceptionally difficult to create. For a human, 110,000 hairs have to be animated. For Remy, 1.15 million hairs had to be animated.

701.   Marketing tie-ins for the film were very difficult because no food company wanted to associate with a rat.

702.   The animators had pet rats for a year during production so they could study their movements.

703.   PIXAR were afraid no one would know how to pronounce Ratatouille so the

phonetic pronunciation was on all posters and trailers.

704. The room that Anton Ego writes his review in is shaped like a coffin.

705. Auguste Gusteau's name means "lord of taste."

706. Auguste Gusteau's first name is an anagram of his surname.

707. The French waiter who talks about cheese is voiced by the director, Brad Bird.

708. The DVD includes the short, Your Friend the Rat.

The Rescuers
1977

709.   This was the first Disney film to have a sequel. The Rescuers Down Under was released in 1990.

710.   Despite the fact that Walt Disney died eleven years before the film's release, he had a lot of input in the story because he had begun working on it in 1962, four years before his death.

711.   Medusa's pet alligators are called Brutus and Nero.

712.   Upon its release, some viewers complained that the film art looks lazy and sketchy. This art technique was intentional and was also used for The Sword in the Stone.

713.   A Mickey Mouse watch appears on the wall of the Rescue Aid Society building.

714.   Although the owl's name is never mentioned in the film, he is called Deacon.

715.   The rabbit is called Deadeye.

716.   Walter Matthau was supposed to play the lead, Bernard.

717.   The albatross is called Orville. He is named after Orville Wright, who invented the first plane with his brother, Wilbur.

718.   Penny freezes every time she looks at Madame Medusa. This is a reference to the Greek mythological creature, Medusa the Gorgon.

Rescuers Down Under
1990

719.   This was the first digital feature film ever made.

720.   Clint Eastwood was considered for McLeach.

721.   Dan Aykroyd was considered for Wilbur.

722.   Steve Martin was considered for a role.

723.   Cody is derived from the Irish word "cuidigtheach" which means "guardian."

724.   Apart from PIXAR films, this is the last animated Disney sequel that was theatrically released.

725.   The Prince and the Pauper was shown in cinemas before this film.

726.   There are no songs in the film.

727.   This was supposed to have a sequel but one of the main actors died so that idea was scrapped.

Road to El Doraldo
2000

728. The sacred book has a picture of a man fishing from the moon. This is a reference to the DreamWorks logo.

729. This was the only animated film that DreamWorks made that didn't make a profit.

730. The armadillo is called Bibo.

731. The Spanish general is called Cortes. In real life, his name was Gonzalo Pizarro.

732. Antonio Banderas turned down the lead role, Tulio.

733. The original title was City of Gold.

734. The film was based on Rudyard Kipling's story, The Man Who Would Be King.

Robin Hood
1973

735.   Friar Tuck was originally going to be a pig.

736.   Five of the actors in this were also in The Aristocats.

737.   This film started as the European fable, Reynard the Fox.

738.   This was the first Disney film to have anthropomorphic animals (animals with human characteristics) without any human characters.

739.   To save money and time, the dancing in the woods scenes was copied frame-by-frame from the dance scene in Snow White and the Seven Dwarves.

Robots
2005

740.   This was directed by Chris Wedge. He is
        most famous for playing Scrat from the Ice
        Ages series.

741.   According to the director, if Robin
        Williams had to do a scene ten times, he
        would usually try it in ten different accents.

742.   This was the first animated film Robin
        Williams did since Aladdin and the King of
        Thieves.

743.   On Fender's, Map of the Stars Homes, it
        reads – Jeremy Iron, Orson Wheels, Axle
        Roses, Britney Gears, Farrah Faucet and M.C.
        Hammer.

744.   This was originally going to be a
        musical.

The Secret of NIMH
1982

745.   In the novel that this story is based on, the main character is called Mrs. Frisby. In the film, her name was changed to Mrs. Brisby to avoid legal ramifications from the Frisbee company, Wham-O.

746.   The director was Don Bluth. He left Disney to make this film. It was rejected by Disney for being "too dark." After it did well, twenty Disney animators left the company. They were known as the Disney Defectors.

747.   The dragonfly Mr. Ages chases in the beginning of the film is Evinrude, the same dragonfly from The Rescuers.

748.   This is Will Wheaton's film debut.

749.   The sword fight at the end was almost entirely copied from the climactic scene in The Adventures of Robin Hood.

750.   At the time, this was the biggest animated film ever that was not made by Disney.

751. The film has many supernatural elements. These aspects do not exist in the original novel.

Shaun the Sheep
2015

752.   It took six years to make this film.

753.   The stop-motion animation was so painstaking, that the animators could only produce two seconds of footage per day.

754.   Twenty animators worked on this film.

755.   There is no dialogue whatsoever.

756.   It was released on the Chinese New Year's Day. This is the Year of the Sheep.

757.   One of the cat's in Animal Control has a mask like Hannibal Lecter.

758.   Shaun's bag has a Blue Peter badge.

759.   When the Farmer is called Mr. X, he poses exactly like Wolverine from the X-Men series. Wolverine is also known as Weapon X.

760.   The Farmer's farm is called Mossy Bottom Farm.

Shrek
2001

761.   Nicholas Cage was offered the part of Shrek but he turned it down. He said it is one of the biggest regrets of his career.

762.   Chris Farley was cast as Shrek and had recorded most of his lines before he suddenly died. He was replaced by Michael Myers.

763.   Mike Myers performed Shrek in a neutral voice. As time went by, he realised that the voice didn't sound right coming out of Shrek's mouth. He insisted that Shrek would have a working class accent. He demanded to re-record all of his dialogue in a Scottish accent. This means the animators would have to reconfigure how Shrek's mouth moved in every scene. Some sources say that this cost the film and extra $4 million but this is not true.

764.   The accent Mike Myers uses for Shrek is how his mother spoke to him as a child when she read him bedtime stories.

765.   "Shrek" is Yiddish for "monster."

766. Mike Myers uses the same Scottish accent for the Austin Powers films.

767. None of the actors met until the film was finished.

768. Steven Spielberg nearly made the film in 1991.

769. To make Shrek's love scene more convincing, Mike Myers recorded his lines to his wife, Robin Ruzan.

770. Eddie Murphy was nominated for a BAFTA for his role as Donkey.

771. The Gingerbread Man is called Gingy.

772. Shrek showering in mud was the hardest scene to animate.

773. Cameron Diaz based Princess Fiona on her sister.

774. The villain, Lord Farquaad, was based on the former Disney CEO, Michael Eisner.

775. When Fiona asks Shrek and Donkey about Lord Farquaad, they keep making references to how short he is. However, when they met him, there was no way they could see that he was a dwarf.

776. Over a thousand characters invade Shrek's swamp near the beginning.

777. Everything in Farquaad's castle is angular. Nothing has curves or bends.

778. Robin Williams was considered for Donkey.

779. Farquaad's logo is very similar to the Facebook logo.

Shrek 2
2004

780. Princess Fiona has a poster of Sir Justin Timberlake. When the animators came up with this idea, they had no idea that Cameron Diaz was dating Justin Timberlake.

781. This is the first animated sequel to be nominated for an Oscar for Best Animated Feature.

782. Antonio Banderas does the voice of Puss. He also does the voice in the Spanish and Italian version.

783. In Far Far Away, there is a restaurant called Burger Prince. This is an obvious reference to Burger King.

784. Mongo has the same roar as Godzilla.

785. Shrek's face has 218 working muscles.

786. When Puss is thrown off of Donkey, he screams in Spanish. It translates into, "How dare you do this to me, you four-legged bag of meat!"

787.   Jennifer Saunders voices the villain, The Fairy Godmother. She performed her own singing.

788.   This was the highest grossing film of 2004.

789.   In the original script, the Dragon was going to turn into Pegasus after it drank the potion.

790.   One of the women who flirts with Shrek says she will "fetch a pail of water." She is later referred to as "Jill."

791.   William Steig was the writer of the Shrek story. He died during production. The film is dedicated to him.

792.   Hair is so difficult to animate, that a wig weaver visited DreamWorks studio to explain how he makes hair look realistic.

793.   The director said that the film, Guess Who's Coming to Dinner? was a massive inspiration to the story

794.   The entrance to Far Far Away is similar to the entrance of Paramount Studios.

Shrek the Third
2007

795.   Dragon and Donkey's children are called Bananas, Parfait, Peanut, Debbie and Coco.

796.   It took 150 crew-members to make this film.

797.   Each tree in this film has 62,173 branches. Every tree has 191,545 leaves.

798.   1,373 characters were created for the theatre scene.

799.   The film was shipped to cinemas under the fake title, Stone.

800.   One million man-hours went into making this film.

Shrek Forever After
2010

801.   Rumpelstiltskin is the villain of this story. He briefly appeared in Shrek the Third but he looked dramatically different.

802.   When Eddie Murphy heard the title, he thought it was a joke because it sounded awful.

803.   One of Rumpelstiltskin's witches is called Baba. She is a witch from Russia mythology called Baba Yaga.

804.   The story revolves around Shrek and Fiona having marriage problems. To make this look realistic, the studio consulted marriage counsellors for advice.

805.   The original title was Shrek Goes Fourth.

The Simpsons Movie
2007

806.   The film had 158 drafts.

807.   The script was so secret, that it was shredded after every voicing session.

808.   Homer calls his pig, Spider-Pig. This is a reference to a character in Marvel Comics called Spider-Ham. His civilian name is Peter Porker.

809.   Marge was supposed to have the vision in the beginning instead of Abe.

810.   20th Century Fox registered the website simpsonsmovie.com in 1997, nine years before the film was green-lit.

811.   The film was sent to cinemas under the codename, Yellow Harvest. This is a reference to Star Wars: Episode VI - Return of the Jedi, which was sent to cinemas under the name, Blue Harvest.

812.   Julie Kavner had to do the "Goodbye Homie" scene over a hundred times.

813.   Moe's Tavern is called Moe's Bar in the film.

814.   Only one joke from the first draft made it into the final cut.

815.   When the Simpsons enter Alaska, the border guard gives them $1000. Alaska actually does this but only if the citizen resides there for at least a year and doesn't have a criminal record.

Sleeping Beauty
1959

816.   In the original German story, Sleeping Beauty is called Briar Rose. In this film (and the Italian version of the story,) she's known as Aurora.

817.   Aurora's body is based on Audrey Hepburn.

818.   Aurora only has eighteen lines.

819.   Maleficent's raven is called Diablo.

820.   When the dragon snaps its jaws, the sound effect is actually a castanet.

821.   The clouds above Maleficent's castle are in the shape of skulls.

822.   Prince Philip and Aurora waltz in the film. The waltz didn't exist until the 16th century but the film takes place in the 14th century. At this time, it was common for couples to perform line-dancing.

Snow White and the Seven Dwarfs
1937

823.   Walt Disney couldn't decide what to make for his first animated feature film – Snow White and the Seven Dwarfs or A Princess of Mars. A Princess of Mars was eventually made in the Disney film, John Carter. It is the most unsuccessful film in Disney history and lost nearly $200 million.

824.   The original title was Seven Little Men Help a Girl.

825.   In the original story, none of the dwarves are named.

826.   A scene was cut which shows the dwarves singing at the kitchen table. This scene can be watched on YouTube.

827.   The animators didn't like the use of the word "dopey" as it sounded too modern in a timeless fairy-tale. Walt Disney corrected them by saying that the word "dopey" was used in a Shakespeare play. The animators accepted the word "Dopey" after this... even though it is completely untrue.

828.   Twenty-five songs were written for the film. Eight were used.

829.   When Snow White kisses the dwarves goodbye, for some reason, she doesn't kiss Sleepy.

830.   This was the first animated feature ever made. Because it had never been done before, many people were certain it would fail.

831.   Other names considered for the dwarves were Blabby, Dirty, Gaspy, Gloomy, Hoppy, Jumpy and Shifty.

832.   Lucilla La Verne played the Wicked Queen. The first time she did the Old Witch voice, the animators were astounded by how different she sounded. They asked her how she did that voice. She said, "Oh, I just took my teeth out."

South Park: Bigger, Longer and Uncut
1997

833.   Paramount asked the writers, Trey Parker and Matt Stone, if they could make the film PG-13. The writers said if they did, it wouldn't be South Park.

834.   This film marked the first time that Kenny's face is seen.

835.   At the time of its release, this film had the world record for the most offensive words and gestures. The film contains 399 swear words, 199 offensive gestures and 221 acts of violence. Trey Parker and Matt Stone intentionally made the film have 399 swear words because they knew it would be X-rated if it had 400.

836.   The song, Blame Canada, was nominated for an Oscar. Robin Williams sang it at the award ceremony.

837.   In the credits, it says the Satan was played by himself.

838.   This is the most successful R-rated animation ever.

839. Trey Parker said the biggest influence on the story was Les Miserables.

840. Chris Rock said that this is the funniest film he has ever seen.

841. There is a poster in the cinema for Mecha Streisand Takes New York. This is a parody of Barbara Streisand (who the directors detest) and the film, Godzilla vs Mecha Godzilla.

842. When Kenny goes to hell, he is greeted by Hitler, George Burns and Gandhi.

843. The final fight is modelled after Dragon Ball Z.

844. Stan barely swears in the film.

845. Heaven has a population of 1,656. Hell has a population of just under a trillion.

The Sword in the Stone
1963

846.   Merlin's crankiness and playful manner were based on Walt Disney. Merlin even has the same nose as Walt. Walt didn't know this until the film was released.

847.   Three actors voice Arthur.

848.   This was the first Disney film to be made by a single director.

849.   Apart from the prologue, the Sword in the Stone doesn't appear for seventy-one minutes, eight minutes before the film ends.

850.   The film concludes with a battle between Merlin and Mad Madam Mim. They attack each other by transforming into several different animals. Most animators say this scene is one of the most significant scenes in animated history. In fact, many new animators study this scene to see how to animate a creature but maintain its character with easily definable features. Every animal that Merlin turns into looks gentle and every animal that Mim turns into looks evil.

Tangled
2010

851. Idina Menzel auditioned for Rapunzel but the producers didn't think her singing was good enough. Shortly after, she was cast as Elsa in Frozen.

852. The original title was Rapunzel.

853. This film is, by far, the most expensive animated film ever, costing $260 million.

854. This is longest Disney film since Fantasia.

855. Rapunzel's parents never speak.

856. Gothel wears a Renaissance dress from the 1780s. This suggests that she was born in this time.

857. 45,000 lanterns appear in the I See the Light scene.

858. Rapunzel is the first Disney princess with supernatural powers.

859.   Maximus' is most people's favourite character even though he has no dialogue.

860.   There are 3,000 people in the Kingdom Dance scene. This is the most animated characters in one scene in a Disney film.

861.   Kristin Bell auditioned for the lead. She was eventually cast as Anna in Frozen.

862.   Flynn was going to be called Bastian.

863.   David Schwimmer was cast in a role but his scene was removed.

864.   This is the first CGI fairy-tale film by Disney.

865.   Natalie Portman was considered for the lead role.

866.   Reese Witherspoon was the first choice for Rapunzel but she wasn't available.

867.   Gothel's appearance is based on Cher.

868.   This was the fiftieth animated film by Disney.

Tarzan
1999

869.   The explorer's camp has a kettle pot that looks like Mrs. Potts from Beauty and the Beast.

870.   Brian Blessed plays the villain, Clayton. He also did the famous Tarzan yodel.

871.   The way Tarzan moves among the trees is based on the movements of pro skateboarder, Tony Hawk.

872.   The ship wreck occurs in 1888. The rest of the story takes place in 1911.

873.   An anatomical professor had to speak with the animators to get an accurate idea of how Tarzan's body would look if he was supposed to depict a person at his absolute physical peak.

874.   The story is set in Kenya.

875.   Harrison Ford was considered for Kerchak.

876.   Ian McKellen was considered for the villain.

877.   Tarzan has been adapted more than any story apart from Dracula.

878.   Of all the Tarzan films that exist, this is the only one to have a one-word title.

879.   Brian Blessed said that Clayton is the best character he has ever played.

TMNT
2007

880.   Leonardo, Raphael and Donatello have brown eyes. Michelangelo was given blue eyes to make him appear younger and more innocent.

881.   Some of the monsters are based on mythological beasts including the Yeti, the Cyclops, a gargoyle and the Jersey Devil.

882.   Mako played Splinter. Although he is not well-known in the Western world, he has a cult following and is considered to be one of the most respectable actors in Japanese history.

883.   It was publically announced that Mako would star in the film the day before he died.

884.   This was Mako's last film.

Toy Story
1995

885.   When the director, John Lasseter, showed the script to the producers in 1993, it was a disaster. Woody was seen as an arrogant jerk and Buzz Lightyear was annoyingly stupid. Lasseter was certain that the producers would pull the plug on the whole film. Luckily, he was given another chance.

886.   If you type in Toy Story Test Footage in YouTube, you can watch the very first animation that was created for the film.

887.   Mickey Mouse can be seen as one of the clouds in Andy's wall at the start of the film.

888.   Buzz Lightyear's name is based on Buzz Aldrin.

889.   Weezy the penguin was supposed to be in this film. He debuted in the sequel.

890.   In Andy's room, there are books on the shelf called Tin Toy, Knick Knack, Red's Dream and Luxo Jr. These are the names of

animated shorts made by PIXAR in the 1980s.

891.   None of the toys close their eyes in unison.

892.   Jim Carrey was the first choice to play Buzz.

893.   Although it's never said at any point, Andy's surname is Davis.

894.   When Andy and his mom head to the pizza place, they stop at Dinoco for fuel. Dinoco is a company in the film, Cars. It is the company that the Lightning McQueen is obsessed with.

895.   When Buzz is dressed as Mrs. Nesbit, he refers to the two headless dolls as "Marie-Antoinette and her little sister." Marie-Antoinette was a French queen that got her head cut off.

896.   Bob Dylan was supposed to write the music for the film.

897.   Bill Murray was considered for the role of Buzz Lightyear.

898.   When Woody dunks his head into a bowl of cereal, no milk spills out because the animators couldn't animate liquid properly at the time.

Toy Story 2
1999

899.   The short, Luxo Jr., was shown in the cinema before this film.

900.   Most of the editors worked 36-48 hour shifts during the production of this film.

901.   During the making of this film, some of the animators would suddenly burst into tears from pure exhaustion.

902.   Woody's nightmare, the yard sale and the Buzz Lightyear video game were all supposed to be in the first film.

903.   The characters in Woody's Roundup look like puppets on strings. In reality, they are computer generated.

904.   Al never says "Woody" once, even though he's obsessed with him.

905.   At one point, Buzz tells Woody, "You are a toy!" This is a reference to when Woody said this to Buzz in the first film.

906.   This is the first sequel that Tom Hanks ever did.

907.   The airport baggage scene was the most complex scene to animate. It took 72 hours to render a single frame.

908.   When Buzz Lightyear is arrested by the other Buzz, he says, "You are in direct violation of Code 6404.5" This is a law in California that bans smoking in public places.

909.   In the original script, Bullseye could talk.

910.   There are many subtle references to the Star Wars franchise (and a few unsubtle ones.)

911.   Mr. Potato Head stops a door from closing by hurling his hat at it like a Frisbee. When he does this, he performs the same motion as Oddjob from the film, Goldfinger, when he throws his hat.

912.   Wheezy the penguin is based on Linux's mascot, Tux.

913.   Rex plays the Buzz Lightyear game on a Super Nintendo.

914.   Al's surname is McWhiggin.

915.   The old man that fixes Woody's arm is called Geri. He was in the PIXAR short, Geri's Game.

Toy Story 3
2010

916.   The short, Day & Night, was shown in the cinemas before this film.

917.   The Western at the beginning was supposed to be in the first film.

918.   The animators said that they watched "pretty much every prison movie" to prepare for the film. The animators found Cool Hand Luke to be the most inspirational film.

919.   Bonnie's surname is Anderson.

920.   The director had his son, Max, draw Daisy's name on Big Baby's pendant.

921.   At one point, Barbie says, "Authority should derive from the consent of the governed, not from the threat of force!" This is an exact quote from the Declaration of Independence.

922.   One of Ken's suits is a Nehru, famously worn by the Bond villain, Blofeld, in You Only Live Twice.

923. Lotso was originally going to be a Care Bear.

924. There are 302 characters in this film.

925. This is the only film where Andy says the names of his toy.

Transformers: The Movie
1986

926. This film is set twenty years after the second season of the television show.

927. The film had a surprisingly good cast including Leonard Nimoy, Eric Idle, Judd Nelson, Casey Kasem and Orson Welles.

928. In some countries, the film is called Transformers Apocalypse! Matrix Forever!

929. Megatron is voiced by Frank Welker. Although many people have never heard of the actor, he is considered to be one of the greatest voice-over actor of all time. He has over 750 acting credits to his name.

930. Many characters died so that the company, Hasbro, had an excuse to bring out lots of new toys.

931. Orson Welles played the villain, Unicron. When Welles was asked what the film was about, he said, "I play a big toy who attacks a bunch of smaller toys."

932. The film is set in 2005.

933.   Fourteen Transformers die in this film.

934.   When Unicron roars, the sound is actually from the Hulk in the 1982 cartoon series.

935.   Unicron was originally going to be called Ingestor.

936.   In the original script, the Transformers planet, Cybertron, was going to turn into a robot and fight Unicron.

937.   Orson Welles was so ill when he did his voiceover work, that some have suggested Leonard Nimoy voiced his scenes. This is not true.

938.   This was the last film Orson Welles ever made.

Treasure Planet
2002

939.   This film took ten years to make.

940.   The lead, Jim Hawkins, was based on
       James Dean.

941.   Jim has a Stitch doll on his bookshelf.

942.   This film lost more money than any
       other Disney animation - $79 million.

943.   The look of the film was based on an oil
       painting.

944.   This is Disney's third adaption of the
       story, Treasure Island. Disney released
       Treasure Island in 1950 and Muppet
       Treasure island in 1996.

945.   Jim's clothes get lighter as the story
       progresses.

Up
2009

946.   The short, Partly Cloudy, was shown in the cinema before this film.

947.   Bob Peterson does the voice of the stupid dog, Dug, and the dog leader, Alpha.

948.   Bob Peterson modelled his character, Dug, from his time as a camp counsellor.

949.   The heroes of the film were drawn with circles and rectangles. Carl has a rectangular head and glasses. Russell has a round face and body.

950.   The villains of the film all have triangular shapes on their face (pointy ears, noses, mouth, etc.)

951.   Carl and Ellie picnic under the tree from the film, A Bug's Life.

952.   When Charles Muntz says he will return with the beast alive, the animators didn't create an audience. Muntz is literally talking to a bunch of hats. The animators did this to save time.

953.   20,622 balloons are used to lift Carl's house.

954.   It would take 12,658,392 balloons to actually lift Carl's house in real life.

955.   This is the first Disney film to mention a divorce.

956.   Ellie is played by Elie Docter. She is the director's daughter.

957.   The DVD includes the short, Dug's Special Mission.

Wallace and Gromit:
Curse of the Were-Rabbit
2005

958.   The film needed 2.8 tons of Plasticine to make all of the character models.

959.   1,000 baby-wipes were needed every week to wipe the Plasticine off the animators' fingers.

960.   Straight after the film was released, the animators warehouse burned down, destroying all of the character models.

961.   The animators managed three seconds of footage per day.

962.   It took five years to make this film.

963.   In the year 2005, two stop-motion films were released – this and Corpse Bride. Helena Bonham Carter starred in both.

964.   The Were-Rabbit attacks a shop called Harvey's. This is a reference to the film, Harvey, which is about a man who is friends with a gigantic rabbit.

965.   Cheese sales skyrocketed during the release of this film.

966.   Vegetable themed posters can be seen in the town like Carrot on a Hot Tin Roof and Spartichoke.

967.   Wallace is based on the director's father.

968.   Thirty sets were built for this film.

969.   44lbs of glue had to be used every month to keep the sets stuck down.

970.   Ray Harryhausen visited the set. He is the greatest stop-motion director of all time.

971.   Forty-three versions of Gromit and thirty-five versions of Wallace had to be created for the film.

972.   250 people worked on the film.

WALL-E
2008

973.   The short, Presto, was shown in the
       cinemas before this film.

974.   The film's working title was Trash
       Planet.

975.   Ben Burtt plays 80% of the cast. He
       personally recorded 2,500 sound effects for
       the film.

976.   WALL-E's name is a reference to Walt
       Disney. His full name is Walter Elias Disney.

977.   This story takes place in 2805 A.D.

978.   WALL-E stands for "Waste Allocation
       Load Lifter - Earthclass."

979.   EVE stands for "Extra-terrestrial
       Vegetation Evaluator."

980.   The ship is called the Axiom. An axiom is
       a part of math that is absolute or taken for
       granted.

981.   The Axiom's paths are color-coded; the blue ones are for humans, the white ones are for robots and the red ones are for stewards.

982.   The DVD has a short called BURN-E, that shows the adventures of a robot on the Axiom.

983.   Most PIXAR films require 75,000 storyboards. This film needed 125,000.

984.   The PIXAR team had to watch every Charlie Chaplin and Buster Keaton film every day during lunch for eighteen months. This was to help them be able to tell a story without dialogue.

Watership Down
1978

985.   This is considered to be the most violent animated PG-rated film ever.

986.   The British Board of Film Classification still receive complaints for this film nearly forty years after it was released.

987.   The film is based in Hampshire, England.

988.   The film is based on the 1972 novel of the same name. It was written by Richard Adams.

989.   John Hurt plays the lead character, Hazel. He also played the villain, Woundwort, in a 1999 remake.

Wreck-It Ralph
2012

990.   The short, Paperman, was shown in the cinema before this film.

991.   The studio said that Nintendo were very particular about how their characters were portrayed. During the Bad Guy meeting, one Nintendo executive said, "Bowser would NEVER hold a tea cup like that!"

992.   Zangief from Street Fighter attends the Bad Guy meeting, even though he is a hero in the video game.

993.   This is the first Disney film to show gun violence since Atlantis: The Lost Empire.

994.   Kano from Mortal Kombat performs his finishing move during the Bad Guy meeting.

995.   Originally, most of the characters (including Ralph) were going to look 8-bit.

996.   Ralph and Fix-It Felix are based on Donkey Kong and Jumpman from the Arcade game, Donkey Kong.

997. The developers were trying to find a way to incorporate Super Mario in the story. After a while, they gave up because they didn't want to put him in the film just for the sake of it.

998. When Fix-It-Felix jumps, he makes the same sound as Mario when he jumps in Super Mario RPG.

999. King Candy's safe is locked with a NES controller.

1000. King Candy's password is Up, Up, Down, Down, Left, Right, Left, Right, B, A, Start. This is one of the most famous cheats in any game in history. It was a cheat in the Konami game, Contra.

Printed in Great Britain
by Amazon